'The second edition of *Helping Your Transgender Teen* seamlessly incorporates today's evolving use of non-binary language to keep the book fresh and relevant. What hasn't changed, thankfully, is author Irwin Krieger's gentle and highly knowledgeable approach in presenting basic information about transition, while delivering the comforting message parents most need to hear: that their kid is going to be OK, and so will they.'

—*Rachel Pepper, LMFT, author of* Transitions of the Heart

'Irwin Krieger has given parents the gift of a brilliant, empathic roadmap in their journey with their transgender teen. He stretches our horizons to bring into focus not just youth who tell us "I'm the opposite gender" but non-binary youth who identify as neither male nor female, but both or all. Elegant, streamlined, and robust, a must-read for anyone raising or promoting the gender health of a transgender teen.'

—*Diane Ehrensaft, Ph.D., author of* The Gender Creative Child *and Director of Child and Adolescent Gender Center, University of California San Francisco*

'Like Irwin himself, this book is accessible, informative, and helpful for parents and anyone who cares about a transgender, non-binary, or gender creative child or teenager. Irwin's down-to-earth explanations, examples, and recommendations bring the material to life and provide concrete, manageable ideas for parents and other caregivers looking for guidance. He has a unique ability to make the complex clear, especially for parents who are negotiating the nuances of the growing number of youth holding non-binary identities.'

—*Robin P. McHaelen, MSW, Executive Director, True Colors, Inc.*

Helping Your Transgender Teen
2nd Edition

A GUIDE FOR PARENTS

Irwin Krieger

Jessica Kingsley *Publishers*
London and Philadelphia

Disclaimer: The information and suggestions contained in this book are not intended as a substitute for consulting directly with a mental health clinician. All matters regarding your child's physical and mental health require professional supervision. The author and publisher shall not be liable or responsible for any loss or damage caused or allegedly caused by any information or suggestion in this book.

First published in 2011 by Genderwise Press
This edition first published in 2018
by Jessica Kingsley Publishers
73 Collier Street
London N1 9BE, UK
and
400 Market Street, Suite 400
Philadelphia, PA 19106, USA

www.jkp.com

Copyright © Irwin Krieger 2011, 2018

Library of Congress Cataloging in Publication Data
A CIP catalog record for this book is available from the Library of Congress

British Library Cataloguing in Publication Data
A CIP catalogue record for this book is available from the British Library

ISBN 978 1 78592 801 7
eISBN 978 1 78450 819 7

Printed and bound in the United States

For my parents, Nava and Elbie,
in appreciation of your love and tenacity during
my own youthful push for authenticity.

Acknowledgments

Thanks to the teens and parents who put their trust in me and taught me so much; to my partner, John Mayer, for your patience, support and encouragement, and for your astute advice through multiple drafts of this book; to Alan Krieger, Sena Messer, Lisa Taylor, and Sharon Laura for your helpful suggestions and revisions for the first edition; and to Lois Spivack, for your help and guidance in my work with transgender clients.

Thanks to Francie Mandel for your outstanding conferences at Boston Children's Hospital, and your continued enthusiastic endorsement of my work; to Susan Maasch for being an early and outspoken fan of *Helping Your Transgender Teen*; and to Pat Jenkins for the best testimonial a book could ever want, at WPATH in 2011. You are the best confidence boosters an author could ask for.

Thanks to Bobbi Mark, for urging me to entrust my self-published book to a professional publisher, and to Andrew James, Alexandra Holmes, Yojaira Cordero, Emily Badger, and the staff at Jessica Kingsley Publishers for being so easy to work with.

Contents

Each of us deserves the freedom to pursue
our own version of happiness;
to make the most of our talents; to speak our minds; to not fit in;
most of all, to be true to ourselves.
That's the freedom that enriches all of us.

PRESIDENT BARACK OBAMA,
FOR THE 'IT GETS BETTER' PROJECT[1]

---

1   Accessed on 7/31/17 at https://obamawhitehouse.archives.gov/it-gets-better-transcript

Preface to the Second Edition

Much has changed since I began writing *Helping Your Transgender Teen* in 2010. Since that time there has been a tremendous increase in the visibility of transgender people in a variety of media, including many recently published memoirs. The number of YouTube videos of transgender teens sharing their experiences has grown dramatically. *Transparent* premiered on Amazon in 2015, winning awards and a large following. Many transgender people are involved in its production. *Billions* on Showtime introduced a character with a non-binary gender identity in 2017. The actor playing this role identifies as non-binary. There are reality shows and numerous documentaries showing the struggles and joys of transgender people and their families. Many of them are about the families of transgender teens and children.

In the United States, under President Barack Obama, the Department of Justice and the Department of Education issued guidelines instructing schools to respect the rights of transgender students. Even though the guidelines were rescinded by the current politically conservative administration, the laws upon which the guidelines were based are still in force.[1] Many high

---

1   Title IX requires gender equity for boys and girls in every educational program that receives U.S. government funding. The Family Educational Rights and Privacy Act (FERPA) protects the privacy of student education records.

schools have more than one student who has come out as transgender. In 2017, the Williams Institute at the UCLA School of Law estimated that approximately 0.7 percent of teenagers in the U.S., aged 13 to 17, identify as transgender.[2]

In 2013, the Maine High Court ruled that schools in Maine must allow a transgender student to use the bathroom that matches their gender identity. Many colleges now include discussion of gender identity in their student orientations. Eighteen U.S. states and the District of Columbia have laws regarding transgender rights as of 2017. Most were passed in the last few years. More families in the U.S. have insurance coverage that includes transgender health care.

All of these changes show that Americans are increasingly aware of and accepting of transgender people. In most places in the U.S., transgender people are better able to live their lives authentically and receive fair treatment than they were seven years ago. Of course, there is still a long way to go before we reach full acceptance and equal legal rights for transgender individuals.

At the same time that all these changes have occurred, there has also been a significant increase in teens coming out with non-binary gender identities. As I explain in the Introduction, these are teens who identify as neither male nor female, or a blend of the two. This is the change that prompted me to revise and update my book. Prior to 2010, when I began writing the first edition, the only trans people talking to me about non-binary identities were young adults. They were most often college students who sought therapy to explore their sense of being neither male nor female or a little of both. Generally, they met with me for a period of a few

---

2   *Age of Individuals Who Identify as Transgender in the United States.* J.L. Herman, A.R. Flores, T.N.T. Brown, B.D.M. Wilson and K.J. Cronin. The Williams Institute, UCLA School of Law, 2017.

months, appreciated the opportunity to talk about this at length, clarified a few things for themselves and were on their way.

In fact, the first edition of *Helping Your Transgender Teen* included my belief at that time that most teens who come out as transgender are seeking transition from male to female or female to male, while those with non-binary identities 'are more likely to handle this in secret or be seen as rebelling, unconventional or "just going through a phase."'[3] In the years since then, identifying as non-binary has become common among transgender teens. I am revising this book to be helpful to parents whose youth identifies as non-binary, while continuing to include all of the relevant information for parents of teens making a transition from male to female or female to male. Since many teens are uncertain of the exact nature of their transgender identity when they first disclose to parents, you may be reading this book as the parent of a teen who has not determined the specifics of their identity. It is important for you to be aware of the full range of gender identities and the many possible ways your teen's life may unfold.

---

3   *Helping Your Transgender Teen: A Guide for Parents*. Irwin Krieger. Genderwise Press, 2011, p.7.

Introduction

Today's teens have access to a wealth of information about gender identity on the internet. Young people wondering about gender will soon discover what it means to be transgender. They will learn about the experiences of transgender teens and adults and the options people have for changing their body to conform to how they feel inside. Many parents of masculine girls or feminine boys have considered that their child may be gay or lesbian. Usually they do not imagine that their child could be transgender.

How this book will help you

If you are the parent of a transgender teen, this book will help you understand what your child is feeling and experiencing. It will explain what may be in store for you if your child fully embraces being transgender. Most parents do not know anyone who is transgender. They initially approach the subject with tremendous discomfort. It is extremely important as the parent of a transgender child to educate yourself about the variety of gender identities that exist. Be prepared to let go of some of your ideas about what it means to be male or female.

These ideas may have been shaped by your childhood. When you were growing up you learned what it meant to be a boy or a girl. Perhaps what you learned felt right to you and you never gave it much thought. Or perhaps there were times when you felt fenced in by what others expected of you because you were a girl, or because you were a boy. You may have been kept from certain activities or discouraged from pursuing certain interests because of your gender. Most likely by adulthood you figured out how to make your way in the world without questioning whether you are a woman or a man. If you are reading this book, however, someone you care about is struggling with questions about gender.

When teenagers declare they are transgender, parents fear that their child is confused and is choosing a life fraught with danger. As a parent, it is best to be thoughtful, inquisitive and compassionate as you come to understand more about your child's gender identity.

Why I wrote this book

I am a clinical social worker who provided psychotherapy for lesbian, gay, bisexual and transgender (LGBT) individuals and their families for over 30 years. From 2004 onward, my work included more and more transgender teens and their parents. I want to share with you what I have learned from my years of working with these caring and courageous families.

Right now, you may be feeling confused, angry, highly skeptical or completely disbelieving that your child could be transgender. If so, this book is for you. In the next chapter I'll help you understand the words and ideas we use when we talk about gender identity. The following three chapters will highlight gender nonconforming children, the differences between gender and sexuality, and the challenges of adolescence for transgender kids. The remaining chapters will help you address your fears, concerns and uncertainties about your child, so you can be as supportive as possible while your child continues to explore questions about gender identity.

1 The Language of Gender Identity

Let's begin by taking a close look at some of the words we use to describe transgender teens. By understanding various components of a person's identity, we can open a window on the inner lives of teens who question whether they are the boy or girl that others take them to be.

Sex, female or male, is assigned at birth based on the appearance of the baby's genitals. That seems pretty straightforward, and it is for the most part. But a small number of babies are *intersex* – their anatomy is not completely male or female. For our discussion of transgender teens, we will begin with the idea that a person's *assigned sex* is either male or female, based on body structure. But knowing about intersex people reminds us that categories such as male/female, gay/straight, or short/tall generally have an in-between. *Natal sex* is another term that can be used for the sex assigned at birth. A person may be referred to as a *natal female* or a *natal male.*

Gender identity is a person's inner sense of being female, male, neither, or both. Most people have a clear sense of being either male or female and their gender identity conforms to their assigned sex. Rules about how girls and boys should behave are taught to us by our families, peers, schools, books, movies, and other representations in the popular culture. These rules establish certain expectations for each gender.

Gender expression is a person's presentation of self to others as masculine, feminine, neither, or both. The various attributes and behaviors that signal male or female vary somewhat from one national culture or ethnic group to another. Aspects of gender expression include one's manner of movement and speech, ways of dressing and grooming, and certain behaviors and interests that are considered to be acceptable only for girls (such as playing with dolls) or only for boys (such as playing football). Children whose gender presentation does not meet society's (and the family's) expectations for their sex generally are treated with disapproval. They learn quickly to try to change themselves to fit in. *Gender nonconforming* children are those who persist in their preferred behaviors and interests, even when those run counter to what is expected of them as a boy or a girl.

Transgender, or *trans,* is a word that describes a wide variety of individuals. Most people are *cisgender.* This term means that their assigned sex, gender identity and gender expression are all male or all female. But transgender people have a gender identity and/or gender expression that does *not* conform to their assigned sex. Some transgender people identify fully with the sex opposite the one they were assigned at birth. Other trans people have *non-binary gender identities*, being neither male nor female, or a blend of female and male.

People with an in-between gender identity sometimes consider themselves to be *genderfluid* or *genderqueer*, while *agender* or *gender neutral* people may feel they do not have a gender. Some other terms used to describe non-binary identities are *bigender, transmasculine, transfeminine, third gender, pangender and polygender*. See the Glossary for my most current definitions of these terms. Keep in mind that these terms are constantly invented and changing. It is safe to say you cannot assume you know what your child means when they use one of these terms, other than that they are talking about a non-binary gender identity. Ask them what they mean. You'll learn a lot about how they view themself.

You may have noticed my use of the pronoun 'they' in the previous paragraph while referring to one person (your child) rather than a group. I also used the invented word 'themself' instead of the plural 'themselves.' Many non-binary individuals ask to be addressed by 'they' pronouns since they do not want to be referred to as 'he' or 'she.' The pronouns are: they, them, their and themself.

Another group included under the transgender umbrella are people who crossdress. *Crossdressers* wish to adopt the clothing and styles of grooming typical, in their culture, of the other sex. They may or may not question their gender identity. They may or may not feel it is important to appear convincingly as the other sex when they crossdress.

Transsexual is a term that has been used to describe people whose gender identity is in sharp contrast to their assigned sex (as opposed to those with a non-binary identity). This term is now used less often, as it has a clinical sound and emphasizes sex rather than gender.

Many transgender youth are unhappy with aspects of their bodies that do not conform to the gender they feel they are inside. They may be distressed when others assume their gender is the same as their natal sex. You may have heard the term *gender dysphoria*. This term is used to describe the unhappiness or distress caused by the conflict between gender identity and assigned sex or societal expectations for that sex.

A *male-to-female* (MTF) teen was assigned male at birth, is considered by others to be male, but feels she is female. She generally wants to have a more feminine body and to be viewed by others as female. (The use of female pronouns, in this instance, is consistent with how this person feels about herself, despite starting out in life with a male body and appearance.)

A *female-to-male* (FTM) teen was assigned female at birth but feels he is male. He generally wants to have a more masculine body and to be viewed by others as male. (Using the pronouns that correspond to a person's gender identity is a sign of respect.)

Similarly, trans youth with non-binary identities may be described as *male-to-not-male* or *female-to-not-female*. But the teens themselves are likely to use one of the non-binary terms mentioned above or another term that they feel describes their gender more accurately.

Is this getting confusing? Imagine, then, what it is like growing up without any words or role models to explain feeling female but having a male body. Or being told you are a girl when you know inside you are not. Many trans youth grow up feeling different from other kids. They don't fit in. Let's take a look at these gender nonconforming children in the next chapter.

A note on my use of pronouns and gendered words

My aim throughout this book is to use language that is in accordance with a youth's affirmed gender, and I most often use gender neutral language when speaking generally. But as this is a book for parents who are early in the process of learning about transgender identities, in some instances I have used pronouns and words related to the natal sex of a transgender child or teen. This is the language parents start with. I believe this approach helps parents grasp the relevant concepts early on, without having to 'translate' what I'm saying into language they understand. At a number of points in the book I stress the importance of parents using affirming pronouns and words, and I use these pronouns and words more consistently as the book progresses. Parents learn the concepts first and then learn to use affirming language as they continue reading the book.

2 Gender Nonconforming Kids

Gender nonconforming (GNC) kids don't have it easy. They are the girls who won't wear a dress and want to play with the boys. Or the boys who want to play with dolls and don't like rough and tumble activities. GNC kids may like to dress as the opposite sex and take on opposite sex roles in fantasy play. Some GNC boys are teased for feminine mannerisms or high-pitched voices. GNC girls are not interested in jewelry, make-up and frills. They may be interested in cars, trucks and team sports. Girls are less likely to be teased, because they fit in to the socially accepted 'tomboy' role.

Most parents are at ease with a girl who is a tomboy, as long as she conforms to gender expectations at times and grows out of being a tomboy by the time she is a young woman. But the feminine boy is a difficult challenge for his parents. They worry that others will ridicule him, and perhaps think less of them as well. They fear that he is a 'sissy' or a 'momma's boy.' It's hard for some parents to be proud of their feminine son, because of strong cultural taboos. Parents usually encourage these boys to tone down their femininity and pursue more masculine activities. To some extent, parents also encourage their tomboys to embrace more feminine interests.

GNC kids don't fit in easily

GNC kids have a strong sense of not fitting in. At ages when girls play mostly with girls and boys with boys, the GNC child is more comfortable with opposite sex playmates. The boy who plays with girls may be looked down on by his peers and by some adults. The girl who wants to play with the boys may be told, 'No girls allowed!' GNC kids are more likely than gender conforming children to be teased, insulted and rejected by peers and adults. They may sense that they are a disappointment to the adults who matter the most to them, including parents and teachers. They find few role models in the popular culture, and often struggle with low self-esteem. GNC kids who lack social and family support may feel a tremendous sense of shame. They are at great risk of depression, social isolation, self-harm or suicide.[1]

Which GNC kids grow up to be transgender?

Some GNC children grow up comfortable with their assigned sex, while others feel their assigned sex does not fit them. The more strongly gender nonconforming children are the ones who are most likely to be transgender in adulthood.[2,3] Strongly GNC boys are the ones who say out loud that they really are girls or that they were given the wrong body. They may dislike having a penis and sit down when urinating. Strongly GNC girls may believe they

---

1   'Childhood gender nonconformity, bullying victimization, and depressive symptoms across adolescence and early adulthood: An 11-year longitudinal study.' A.L. Roberts, M. Rosario, N. Slopen, J.P. Calzo and S.B. Austin. *Journal of the American Academy of Child and Adolescent Psychiatry*, 52:2, 2013, pp.143–152.

2   *The Gender Creative Child: Pathways for Nurturing and Supporting Children Who Live Outside of Gender Boxes.* Diane Ehrensaft. The Experiment, 2016.

3   'Factors associated with desistence and persistence of childhood gender dysphoria.' T. Steensma, J.K. McGuire, B.P.C. Kreukels, A.J. Beekman and P.T. Cohen-Kettenis. *Journal of the American Academy of Child and Adolescent Psychiatry*, 52:6, 2013, pp.582–590.

will grow up to be men. They may want boys' underwear and short hair. They may express a wish for a penis and dislike developing breasts. They most likely will not celebrate getting their period and becoming women. Strongly GNC boys may feel they should keep their chests covered, always wearing a shirt at the pool or the beach. The girls may want to run around without a shirt on long past the age when parents think it's okay. Children whose strong gender nonconformance persists from year to year are most likely to grow up to be transgender.

Was your teen GNC in childhood?

Think back to when your child was young. Do you recall whether they exhibited many of these gender nonconforming behaviors and desires? Take a look at family photos and videos to see whether your child's public presentation reflected this difference. Do you remember any time they expressed disappointment with gender roles or body parts? If a GNC child makes such a comment and the response is negative, the comment may never be repeated. But the child may continue to feel strongly that there is a mismatch between body and self.

For some parents of transgender teens the situation is not so clear. Perhaps their child who was assigned female was never a tomboy who hated wearing dresses, yet suddenly is a teen declaring he is really a boy. Or there is the child assigned male who seemed in no way different from other boys, yet now says she is a girl inside. Life presents us with endless variations, including the existence of these individuals who seemed comfortable and acted in accordance with their assigned gender in childhood, but now feel strongly that their gender is different. If your child's disclosure that they are transgender seems to come out of the blue, then you will need more time and discussion to gain a full understanding of their inner truth.

3 Sexuality and Gender

So far we've talked about assigned sex and gender but not about sexuality—sexual attractions and sexual behavior. But as we all know, when we're talking about teens, we can't leave out sexuality!

Sexual orientation is not the same as gender

At this point I want to clarify for you that sexual orientation (sexual attraction) is separate from gender identity and gender expression. Some people believe that transgender people are just confused gays or lesbians. Most parents would prefer to find out that their transgender kids are gay or lesbian, rather than transgender. While they face many challenges, gays and lesbians are accepted more easily in our society. The challenges of being transgender are tougher. But just as a person does not choose to be gay or straight, one does not choose to be transgender or cisgender.

Some transgender people do go through a phase of identifying themselves as gay or lesbian. They may already be viewed by others as gay or lesbian because of the stereotype that masculine women are lesbian and feminine men are gay. Before they have the understanding, language and courage to come out as transgender, considering themselves to be gay or lesbian may seem to be the best fit. In this way, many trans people go through the coming out process more than once. They initially accept society's judgment that if they are sexually attracted to people with the same body type then they must be homosexual. Their view changes as they learn about gender identity and gain a new understanding of themselves.

Spectrum of sexual orientations

Once again, this can be confusing, so let me explain it in more detail. Sexual orientation has to do with who we find attractive. Sexual orientation exists across a spectrum. (This was one of the important findings of Kinsey's study of sexuality in the U.S. in the 1940s.[1]) A man may be attracted to only women, mostly women, men and women, mostly men or only men. (And for some people, who may use the term 'pansexual,' gender is not a highly relevant factor in their sexual attractions.) So we can see there is a spectrum from heterosexual to bisexual to homosexual or, in today's language, straight to bi to gay.

If you are certain of your own gender, and aware of your attractions to males and females in varying degrees, you can find your place on this spectrum. Most people in our culture understand themselves to be gay, straight or bisexual, although not all pursue relationships precisely in accordance with their sexual orientation. Societal pressures steer us towards the heterosexual end of the spectrum, so many bisexuals as well as some lesbians and gays present themselves to others as straight. With increasing acceptance of homosexuality as a normal variation in human sexuality, this occurs less often.

---

1   *Sexual Behavior in the Human Male.* A.C. Kinsey, W.B. Pomeroy and C.E. Martin. W.B. Saunders and Co., 1948.

Putting it together: Sexuality and gender

To illustrate these concepts, let's consider a transgender person with a female body and a male gender identity who is attracted to females. If we understand this person to be female, then she is a lesbian. Many female-to-male (FTM) transgender people spend part of their lives being 'out' as lesbian, part of the lesbian community, often fully accepted by friends and family as lesbian. But since the FTM individual truly feels himself to be male and is attracted to females, he identifies as a heterosexual male. If he is able to transition (more about that later) to being male, he will be seen by others as the heterosexual male he is, and not as a lesbian. For him, being lesbian was only a transitional identity on his way to being a straight man.

Of course, some trans people are attracted to both genders and some to the initially 'opposite' sex, so these folks are gay, lesbian or bisexual after transitioning. Here are two fictional examples to help you understand:

Donald and Michelle told me, 'Sam was a quiet, artistic boy, quite different from Melissa, his boisterous older sister. He loved drawing pictures of princesses and fairies. He thoroughly enjoyed dressing in Melissa's clothes and imagining he was "Princess Samantha." Most of his playmates were girls. He occasionally told us he was really a girl. We took that as a sign of his vivid imagination.'

Sam's parents allowed Sam to dress up at home, but not to wear a dress to school. They let Sam grow long hair and never pressured Sam to play sports. They understood that Sam was different from other boys and had trouble fitting in.

In middle school Sam was often teased for being feminine. 'I decided to cut my hair short and join the track team, so I could be one of the guys. The teasing stopped. I realized I was attracted to boys and began to think of myself as gay. But I didn't like the way my body was becoming more masculine. I felt more like a girl inside.'

Sam now attends a support group for LGBT teens. No one there gives Sam a hard time about being feminine. Sam has started dating a gay boy who attends the group, but has not told anyone at school. When Sam thinks of the future, she imagines herself as a woman married to a man. Sam now sees herself as a heterosexual female. Being gay was just a transitional identity for Sam.

According to Tiffany's parents, 'Tiffany was always a bright girl with many interests. She enjoyed friendships with girls and boys. She loved to ski and played saxophone in the school band.' Tiffany told me childhood was a happy time. 'I imagined a future where anything was possible.' Tiffany didn't think much about what was different or special about being a girl.

In puberty, developing breasts and hips didn't feel right. Tiffany was attracted to boys, but didn't like to be viewed as an attractive female. 'I didn't like the feminine sound of my name. I cut my hair short and asked my friends to call me "T.J."'

Now T.J. wears loose clothes to hide his female shape. When he looks in the mirror he is hoping to see a male body looking back. Searching online, T.J. found information about being transgender and realized it applied to him. 'Now I have words to describe how I feel.' T.J. ordered a binder—a garment to safely flatten the breasts and create a more masculine appearance.

With a male gender identity and an attraction to boys, T.J. identifies as a gay boy. We can see him developing into an adult gay male.

I hope these two examples have helped you gain a better understanding of the relationship between sexual orientation and gender identity. It's not important that you sort this out all at once. Your teen will be sorting it out and, hopefully, explaining it to you. All you need to do is keep an open mind and be aware that the possibilities are quite wide ranging. It is helpful to understand that for most transgender people, having the opportunity to present oneself true to one's gender identity is of paramount importance. Concerns about the gender of a sex partner or finding a life mate are secondary. In fact, many transgender teens hold off on dating and intimacy until they are able to sort through and express their gender in a way that feels right for them.

4 Puberty and Adolescence

Gender nonconforming teenagers

What happens to our strongly gender nonconforming kids when they start puberty? Teens who don't look and act like typical boys and girls are likely to bear the brunt of increased harassment. They are presumed to be gay or lesbian, and to the extent that anti-gay feelings are strong in their community, they suffer. For those who *are* lesbian or gay, there may be support from a Gay Straight Alliance at school, or an LGBT Community Center. There are inclusive images of gay and lesbian individuals and families in the mainstream media. Many lesbian and gay teenagers now have the full support of their families and friends.

But what about the kids who appear different and are actually transgender? To date, supports for these kids are absent in most communities. Families are rarely prepared to understand and accept their transgender youth. These kids are most often going through this process alone and in secret. Many are able to seek out information and support on the internet. Few have the in-person support and access to information that they truly need. They may be the only transgender teen present if they attend an LGBT youth group.

When transgender kids reach puberty, their bodies begin to betray them. They develop the physical characteristics that are typical of their assigned sex but not in accord with their deeply felt gender. For example, some transgender girls see cisgender girls developing breasts and feel envious. Any growth of facial hair may be disturbing. Many transgender boys are appalled when their breasts begin to develop. Menstruation can become a monthly reminder of having the wrong puberty.

Two important indicators of transgender identity

There are two important indicators of transgender identity. The first is the discomfort transgender teens feel about the gendered aspects of their bodies, which increase in puberty. When this factor is very strong a youth is more likely to seek medical intervention (see Chapter 8). The second is their desire to be perceived by others as being of the gender they feel they are. For some transgender teens, significant distress about these matters doesn't begin until adolescence. For those whose distress started earlier, the physical changes of puberty usually increase their discomfort. Puberty heightens the physical differences between the sexes. As the body's sexual characteristics become more glaringly obvious with each new development, the discordance with who they are inside becomes more and more disturbing. Comments from others about becoming a young man or a young woman only exacerbate this distress. In childhood, transgender individuals often maintained magical ideas about it all working out in the future. For transgender teens in puberty, this no longer seems possible. As puberty progresses, many begin to feel hopeless about their future.

Despair and isolation

Many transgender adolescents struggle with depression at some point. They may feel hopeless about ever being at ease with who they are. They may believe it is impossible to explain how they feel to their parents and friends. They are likely to fear that disbelief and disappointment will be the response if they choose to do so. They may fear they will lose friends if they share this secret, that word will spread and they will be shunned by all of their peers. Some transgender teens live with the fear that disclosure to family will lead to rejection, physical violence or homelessness.

Some transgender teens dislike looking at themselves in the mirror. Each time they do, these teens are disappointed to see that their outer appearance does not fit with the person they feel themselves to be inside. They may adopt clothes or postures that hide their physical developments, or try to find ways of presenting themselves as neither boy nor girl. They avoid public restrooms, where one has to declare one's gender to enter. They feel out of place in the restroom that coincides with their assigned sex, and look out of place in the one that fits their gender identity. They often avoid pools and beaches where they have to display their body to others.

Trying to fit in

Transgender teens who were consistently gender nonconforming in childhood may make an effort to conform to society's expectations, based on their assigned sex, for some part of their teenage years. This gives them the ability to fit in with peers and get relief from criticism, taunting and the feeling that they are disappointing their parents. Generally, this effort to change one's outer self to please others leads to only a temporary sense of relief. For children who are transgender, at some point the urge to be their authentic self will return full force. For this reason, transgender teens often exhibit mood swings over a period of months or years prior to their disclosure of their transgender identity.

Mental health risks

As a result of these stresses, transgender teens are at risk of serious depression, suicide, self-harming behaviors, substance abuse and low self-esteem. The situation is worse for teens whose differences are not accepted by their families. Research has shown that transgender youths who are rejected by their families have lower self-esteem and are more isolated than youths whose families accept them.[1,2] They have poorer health and higher rates of depression, suicide, substance abuse problems and HIV infection than their peers who report having families and caregivers who support them. Even a little less rejection and a little more family acceptance increases self-esteem, access to social support and life satisfaction, while decreasing the rate of problems. In Chapter 6, I will discuss ways to support and nurture your transgender teen.

As I mentioned above, a teenager's silent inner struggle with gender identity can lead to mood swings. Sometimes the mood swings are viewed by parents and others as typical adolescent emotionality and behavior. When the mood swings persist, the teen may be sent for counseling and/or psychiatric medication. These treatments are largely ineffective if a significant piece of information (the child's gender identity struggle) is missing. The teen's condition will be worse if there is disrespect and harassment due to gender nonconformance. A teen's condition will be most severe if they feel rejected by the family.

1   *Supportive Families, Healthy Children: Helping Families with Lesbian, Gay, Bisexual and Transgender Children.* Caitlin Ryan. Family Acceptance Project, San Francisco State University, 2009.

2   'Impacts of Strong Parental Support for Trans Youth: A Report Prepared for Children's Aid Society of Toronto and Delisle Youth Services.' R. Travers, G. Bauer, J. Pyne, K. Bradley, L. Gale and M. Papadimitriou, 2017. Accessed on 4/25/14 from http://transpulseproject.ca/wp-content/uploads/2012/10/Impacts-of-Strong-Parental-Support-for-Trans-Youth-vFINAL.pdf

Let's look at the story of a transgender teenager who became depressed. While this is a fictional example, it reflects the real-life experience of many of my transgender teen clients.

Cassie was an athletic child, assigned female at birth, with an older brother named Todd. Cassie enjoyed playing football with Todd and his friends. Cassie had little interest in spending time with other girls in the neighborhood. Cassie joined a girls' soccer team and soon became a star player. Cassie was a good student, with an easygoing personality.

As they grew older, Todd and his friends no longer included Cassie in their games. Cassie's feelings were hurt. Cassie's mother, Jen, explained that Todd was getting older and it was natural that he didn't want his little sister tagging along anymore. Jen said Cassie shouldn't take it personally. Todd was still nice to Cassie at other times, but Cassie couldn't help feeling sad and left out.

At school Cassie hung out with friends from the soccer team. In middle school these girls became more interested in how they dressed, wearing makeup, and talking about boys. Cassie was interested in none of these things. It seemed that Cassie didn't fit in anywhere. Jen sensed that Cassie was at an awkward stage. She talked to Cassie about how exciting it could be to become a young woman. She offered to spend some 'girl' time together. They could go shopping or do their nails. She would show Cassie how to put on makeup. Cassie refused. Cassie's father, Rob, wondered if they had made a mistake allowing Cassie to spend so much time with Todd and his friends when Cassie was younger. He told Jen they should have set up more play dates with girls.

Cassie still enjoyed soccer, but felt sad and angry at home and at school. Cassie's grades declined. Friends complained that Cassie was moody. To Jen and Rob it seemed that their easygoing child had suddenly become angry and uncooperative. Some days Cassie refused to go to school. Cassie felt miserable and didn't understand why. A guidance counselor recommended a therapist for Cassie. In therapy, Cassie began to talk about feeling out of place. Cassie didn't fit in with the girls and wasn't included by the boys. Cassie worried about disappointing both parents and friends.

When Cassie felt more comfortable with the therapist, Cassie revealed a fantasy of being a boy named Marcus. In this fantasy Marcus was the captain of the football team. He was dating a popular girl at school. Cassie never imagined being anyone's girlfriend. In fact, Cassie hated the idea of becoming a young woman.

Cassie's therapist had recently attended a conference about LGBT youth. She understood that it is important for teens to be free of others' expectations as they explore their identity. Feeling supported in therapy, Cassie became less angry and moody at home and at school.

As Cassie learned about gay, lesbian, bisexual and transgender identities, Cassie realized he was a transgender boy. Understanding this helped him feel less confused and less alone. He started thinking of himself full-time as 'Marcus.' Marcus found that once he understood and accepted himself, he got along better with his friends and his family. Marcus's grades began to improve.

Jen and Rob were pleased to see improvements in their teen's feelings and behaviors. They were interested to learn what the trouble had been and what had helped make things better. When Marcus told them about being transgender, they had trouble believing it at first. He asked them to start calling him 'Marcus.' When they considered how much better Marcus was feeling since coming to this realization, they tried to be open-minded about it. . Thinking back on Marcus's childhood, they recognized that Marcus had always behaved more like a boy than a girl. This helped them accept that perhaps Marcus's true identity was male.

As in this story, once the child's gender identity is understood and respected, the mental health condition generally improves. In many cases, depression virtually disappears once a teen is feeling fully supported. For this reason, it is extremely important that any mental health assessment and treatment of a gender nonconforming child or teen be provided by a clinician knowledgeable about LGBT youth. See Chapter 7 for information on finding a counselor who is a gender identity specialist.

5 Balancing Authenticity and Safety

Authenticity

Adolescence is a time to figure out who you are. For teens who have realized that their gender identity and their body don't match, being authentically themselves becomes of paramount importance. Their distress about the difference between who they feel they are inside and who they appear to be on the outside increases. They feel stung when others refer to them as the boy or girl they appear to be, rather than who they know themselves to be. They assume, often correctly, that those who care most about them will not be able to accept this aspect of who they really are. They struggle with telling others, perhaps hinting about it at first. They may try out a public identity of lesbian or gay to see how much others can understand and accept.

A teenager who has broken through the fear of disclosure, and has begun to tell parents about being transgender, will often be extremely impatient about making a transition to their affirmed gender. Teens may feel they have been suffering for years, forced to live in the wrong gender role. They cannot understand how difficult it is for parents when the child they view as their daughter is now their son. They do not recognize what a challenge it is for parents to accept a child they thought of as male who suddenly wants to live as female, or to grasp a teen's non-binary identity.

Transgender teens often feel completely certain of their gender identity, and have little or no fear about taking hormones or having surgery. Parents have tremendous fears and concerns. Most often, teens are advocating for immediate full authenticity, while parents advocate for caution and safety, putting the two parties at odds. Let's look at what some of your fears and concerns are likely to be if you are the parent of a transgender teen requesting social transition (living full time in the new gender), hormones and (in the future) surgery.

Confront your fears

Fear of harassment

Perhaps your child has already experienced harassment from peers for being gender nonconforming. As a parent, you expect this will only worsen if your child announces at school that she is a girl, or he is a boy, or they are genderfluid. Of the teens I have worked with (primarily students of public and private high schools in Connecticut), most have not experienced increased harassment when they made a social transition at school. It helped when the student made the social transition with certainty and confidence. If the student can seem at ease about it, others are likely to be more accepting. The student's more open-minded peers will lead the way by treating the teen who has transitioned with respect. See Chapter 7 for more about the social transition at school.

Fear of physical harm

We have all by now heard of tragic incidents in which transgender teens and adults are attacked or killed. Parents worry especially about violence from schoolmates. For this reason, the social transition at school includes meeting with school administration.

Steps are taken to establish a safe and respectful environment for your child at school. If you do not feel that your child can be safe at his or her current school, look for a safe alternative.

As adults involved in the care of transgender teens, we must help them establish as much safety as possible. We must also realize that teens who are not allowed to transition are at increased risk of depression, substance abuse, self-loathing, self-harm or suicide, so refusing the teen's request outright is also a dangerous path. We must work to spread the idea that being transgender is a normal variation in gender identity. This will help over time reduce prejudice and violence against transgender people.

Fear of regret

Parents fear that their teen will have a change of mind after it's too late. They fear that later on in life, their child will feel that taking hormones was a mistake. But experience shows that teens who feel strongly that they are transgender are highly likely to continue feeling that way in adulthood.[1] Research has shown good psychological outcomes in young adulthood for youth who transitioned as teens.[2] Before starting hormones there will be a period of psychotherapy and most likely a social transition. This will allow time for the teen, the parents and those evaluating the teen to be confident before any permanent medical intervention begins.

For teenagers just entering puberty, only fully reversible hormonal interventions are considered. These are hormones that

---

1   'Medical care for gender variant young people: Dealing with the practical problems.' B.W. Reed, P.T. Cohen-Kettinis, T. Reed and N. Spack. *Sexologies*, 17:4, 2008, pp.258–264.

2   'Young adult psychological outcome after puberty suppression and gender reassignment.' A.L.C. de Vries, J.K. McGuire, T.D. Steensma, E.C.F. Wagenaar, T.A.H. Doreleijers and P.T. Cohen-Kettenis. *Pediatrics*, 134:4, 2014, pp. 696–704.

postpone puberty but do not eliminate the option of subsequently going through puberty in accordance with the natal sex. Cross-sex hormones (for a transition to the other sex) will not be considered generally until the teen has had adequate time to attain certainty about the wish to transition. (See Chapter 8 for more information about medical interventions.)

It is also helpful to know that research has shown there is a very low rate of regret among adults who have made a full medical transition.[3] The regrets that do occur are mostly related to poor surgical outcomes, or rejection by family or society. This tells us that the vast majority of the individuals in these studies remained consistent in their belief that their affirmed gender identity is the right one for them.

Examine your concerns

Too young

My child is too young to be certain about something this serious. Parents often recall ideas and interests they had as teens that they no longer hold. They imagine gender identity to be similar to ideas about a career, or raising a family, ideas that generally do change as we mature into young adults (and often throughout our adulthood). Gender identity is more viscerally felt, and more intrinsic to oneself. As a result we can attain a high level of certainty about a teen's gender identity through the process of psychotherapy and through the experience gained from a social transition.

The evaluation of the youth's gender identity includes a number of factors. The therapist examines the development of

---

3   'Eligibility and readiness for sex reassignment surgery: Recommendations for revision of the WPATH *Standards of Care*.' G. DeCyypere and H. Vecruysse, Jr. *International Journal of Transgenderism*, 11:3, 2009, pp.194–205.

gender identity in childhood. Parents provide the therapist with their view of their child's feelings and behaviors at various ages. Teens talk in therapy sessions about their comfort and their struggles through many aspects of growing up. Therapy gives teens an opportunity to speak at length about their sense of self. They discuss in detail their feelings and behaviors related to gender identity. Therapy is an opportunity to talk about any discomfort a youth feels with the gendered aspects of their body, and how they want to be viewed and understood by others. The therapist then monitors the teen's certainty about these feelings over time, including the time of the social transition.

Not really transgender

My child is not transgender but is saying so for one of the following reasons:

- *mental illness*
- *as an emotional reaction to a life trauma or circumstance*
- *to be rebellious*
- *to get attention*
- *to fit in with countercultural friends.*

While any of these explanations may be true in rare cases, generally teens who say they are transgender are transgender, in the general all-inclusive sense of the word. Evaluation by a gender identity specialist (a mental health clinician specializing in gender identity) will clarify those instances in which the child is suffering from a delusion, or asserting a transgender identity out of confusion, to fit in, or to upset parents. These teens' description of their gender identity and their responses to questions from a knowledgeable professional will not be consistent with what we know to be true of transgender individuals. In particular, gender identity specialists can help young people clarify whether or not they want and need to undergo medical transition. Not all transgender youth are seeking medical intervention. Many of those with non-binary identities are seeking simply to be understood, accepted and respected.

Learn as much as you can from your teen about their gender identity development. Below are some good questions to ask. Ask your questions in a spirit of curiosity, without implying criticism or disbelief. Keep an open mind about the validity and meaning of your child's inner experience. Listen, ask for more detail, be patient, and be flexible in your thinking.

- When did you first begin to question your gender identity?
- Do you feel sure now, or are you still questioning?
- How did you fit in with girls and boys when you were younger?
- How do you feel about the male or female aspects of your body?
- How do you feel about the changes to your body that come with puberty?
- How do you feel when people view you as female or male?
- Who have you talked to about this so far and how have they responded?
- Would you like to share this information with other family members?
- Do you want to let people know at school? In your neighborhood? At your internship or job? At your summer camp or summer program?

No need to transition
Nowadays a girl can do anything a boy can do and vice versa. Being transgender is not about gaining access to certain activities or

jobs. Trans people have a deeply felt need to be seen by others as being of the gender they feel inside, and most have a deeply felt discomfort with some or all of the gendered aspects of their body. It can be difficult for parents and other concerned individuals to grasp what this means, as it is an experience unfamiliar to cisgender individuals (those whose assigned sex is the same as their gender identity and expression). It will be important for you to listen closely as your teen explains this important aspect of their inner experience.

Your own discomfort

Most parents do not know anyone who is transgender and initially react to their child's disclosure with discomfort. Parents may have been taught that being transgender is a sickness, immoral, or perverted. It is extremely important as the parent of a transgender child to get free of these negative beliefs. You must educate yourself about the variety of gender identities that exist and open yourself to a full understanding of what is natural and true for your child.

The reactions of others

What will others think? Parents worry about how friends, colleagues, community members and extended family will react to the news that their child is transgender, and some parents are concerned about what others will think of them for having a transgender child. These worries are natural and understandable. But you must not let them get in the way of supporting your transgender child and making decisions in the best interest of your child. Most parents inform only a small number of close friends or family members at first, while the child's gender identity is being discussed and considered. Once a decision has been made for a social transition, parents can consider various options for informing others in person, by phone, by letter or email. It is important to present this new information in a positive light. Explain that you and your child have come to realize something essential about his or her identity. Request that others adopt the new name, corresponding pronouns, and a respectful manner. (This topic is addressed in more detail and with sample letters in Chapter 7.)

When you speak to friends and family, it is important to acknowledge their discomfort and let them know if you felt the same way at first. Tell them that you welcome a chance to respond to any questions or concerns they may have about your child's transition. Ask for their acceptance and support. You will see, if you have not already, that when your child transitions you are making a major transition as well.

Feelings of loss

By the time your child has reached adolescence, you have come to enjoy this boy or girl as someone with a stable gender. Some of your appreciation of your child is connected to your own feelings and assumptions about what it means for the child to be female or male, and what the future holds in store. Despite the notion that we live in a culture where anyone can do anything, regardless of gender, we carry many differing expectations for men and women. These ideas deeply affect our views of who our children are and who they may become. Parents may experience a deep sense of loss when they discover that a child will be changing in outward appearance and identity to conform to a long-felt but previously secret gender identity. It is important for you to have as much time as you need to feel and accept the loss. Talk it over with your spouse or partner, close friends and family, or a trans-friendly mental health professional or clergy member. It may be helpful to let your child know about your feelings of loss, so your teen can understand the ways in which this is a difficult adjustment for you, but it is best not to dwell on this with them. It is not your child's job to help you with this loss. Other supportive adults can do that for you.

The impact on siblings

One final consideration is the concern that many parents have for the siblings of a youth who transitions. In my experience, this generally has not been a problem for siblings who are at least a few years older or younger than the child who is transitioning. But many siblings within a year or two in age worry about peer responses to their sibling transitioning. You should not keep your transgender teen from transitioning in order to make life easier for another child. But it may be helpful to adjust the timing, so the sibling can have a little more time or perhaps an upcoming school break to speak to friends and establish their own supports. For the families I worked with, this type of family planning went smoothly. The transitioning youth understood the need to wait a bit longer for the official transition at school, and the cisgender sibling understood that they can't wait too long. This challenge is more difficult when the community is not supportive of LGBT people. But as a parent you do not have to sacrifice the well-being of one child for another. Instead, get everyone together and figure out a plan that respects the needs of all of your children.

Coming to terms with these fears and concerns

Pay attention to all of these possible fears and concerns, as well as any other troubled feelings you have about your teen's declaration of transgender identity. It is important to address each one that affects you. This will help you prepare to be the best support you can be for your child at this challenging time for all of you. The next chapter will discuss ways to nurture your child at this important juncture in your lives.

6 Nurturing Your Transgender Teen

Keep an open mind

The most helpful thing you can do for your transgender teen is to adopt an open-minded attitude toward whatever they are saying about gender identity and gender expression. Don't be afraid to ask questions. Recognize that it is natural for some parents, who feel they know their child inside and out, to feel that something this significant could not be true for their child yet hidden from them. Remember that the fears and concerns discussed in Chapter 5 may cause you to have a bias against believing that your teen could be transgender. This will be especially the case if your child's behavior until now has been relatively in keeping with society's gender expectations. Accepting that a youth is transgender is easier for parents if that young person is strongly gender nonconforming. Keep in mind that if a parent's first response is to strongly oppose what their teen is saying about gender identity, the youth is more likely to adopt a stubborn and oppositional attitude.

Keep the lines of communication open

A teen who feels you are listening will continue to talk to you. Supportive interaction with your transgender teen reduces the risk of low self-esteem, depression and suicide. It increases the likelihood that your child will let you know of any self-harm or substance abuse. If your teen is engaging in dangerous behavior, seek professional help. Stay as fully engaged as you can with your teen. While teenagers typically pull away from their parents and relate more closely with their peers, transgender teens need their parents' active support. One way to show support and respect is to use the name and pronouns that your teen requests, even if this is difficult for you to do,

Honor your teen's chosen name and pronouns

Some families reach an early impasse over the question of whether and when to use the name and pronouns their child has requested. It is difficult for cisgender parents and other cisgender adults to understand how important this is to a young person's sense of validation and self-worth, which in turn affects their mood and functioning.

Referring to a transgender person by their birth name and pronouns when they have asked you to do otherwise is called 'misgendering.' For many children and teens, being misgendered is painful. It makes them feel invisible. It is an act of disrespect. No one, least of all a loving parent, should fail to provide them with this basic sign of respect.

Honoring your teen's chosen name and pronouns will help them feel better about themself and will improve their relationship with you. It will give them one more opportunity to see if their affirmed gender is right for them. Doing this will not influence a cisgender child to become transgender. It should not be viewed as 'giving in' to a child's whim but as a way of letting them know you support their right to figure out and be their authentic self. I have also found that using the chosen name and pronouns helps remind me of how the young person experiences themself inside, even when their outer appearance reflects their assigned sex. Hopefully, this will also help you understand your child better.

What did I do wrong?

Many parents wonder if they did something wrong in raising their child who turned out to be transgender. *Should I have kept him from playing with dolls and encouraged more rough and tumble activities? Should I have been less enthusiastic about her being such a tomboy? Did I secretly wish she would be a boy because I already had two daughters? Did this happen because there weren't adult men in his life after his father was gone?*

You didn't do anything to cause your child to be transgender! How we interact with our children does not determine their gender identity. Our interactions *do* have an effect on their self-esteem, so it's important to let them know we accept them as they are. You may have made the mistake of criticizing or shaming your child for gender nonconforming behaviors. You may have done so out of fear or ignorance. Now is your opportunity to correct that mistake by expressing your love and support, even when your child's behavior makes you uncomfortable. The Family Acceptance Project's brochure, *Supportive Families, Healthy Children*,[1] gives specific examples of supportive and rejecting behaviors, including some you may not have thought about.

Handle your own discomfort

Many parents are uncomfortable when their teens choose to act or dress in accordance with their affirmed gender identity. It is important to handle your own discomfort. Do not pressure your child to act or dress conventionally for your comfort. Learn to appreciate your teen's uniqueness and courage. This will help you get over any feelings of shame or embarrassment. When

---

1 *Supportive Families, Healthy Children: Helping Families with Lesbian, Gay, Bisexual and Transgender Children*. Caitlin Ryan. Family Acceptance Project, San Francisco State University, 2009. You can download it for free at: https://familyproject.sfsu.edu/publications

transgender teens are harassed by others for their unconventional ways, it is essential for parents to respond with full support. Don't blame your teen for the harassment. All people deserve to live a fully authentic life. If others respond badly, that is not your teen's fault. Your role as a parent is to see what can be done to eliminate or reduce the harassment without sacrificing your child's right to be self-affirming.

If your teen has an autism spectrum disorder (ASD)

Some youth with ASD also identify as transgender. Researchers found that a greater percentage of youth diagnosed with ASD had gender dysphoria when compared to youth without ASD.[2] Parents of autistic children who express a transgender identity often wonder if this is just one of the fixations that some people with ASD have. But these fixated interests tend to be focused on either collections of unusual objects (ones that other children do not typically collect) or overly detailed information on a particular subject.[3] The fixations are about something external to the individual, while gender identity is something a person feels on the inside. Your child's gender identity specialist, with input from you, your teen and any other clinicians working with your child, will help establish the authenticity of your teen's gender identity.

If your teen is on the autism spectrum they may not be very talkative about their gender, even if there are other topics (such as the fixations mentioned above) that they talk about a lot. This may be true in therapy as well. Therefore, the evaluation may take

---

2   'Gender variance among youth with autism spectrum disorders: A retrospective chart review.' A. Janssen, H. Huang and C. Duncan. *Transgender Health*, 1:1, 2016, pp.63-68.

3   *The Complete Guide to Asperger's Syndrome* (revised edition). Tony Attwood. Jessica Kingsley Publishers, 2016.

longer.[4] Your teen may also be less interested in a social transition. Youth who are socially awkward do not like to call attention to themselves. If they are socially isolated, they are unlikely to have a group of friends to accept them in their affirmed gender. But those in special schools or classes may have the benefit of staff who will guide other students to respond supportively.

When your teen has doubts

Even those teens who at times feel certain they are transgender will at other times have some doubts about it. This is not surprising, given society's negative attitudes about transgender people. It is difficult to embrace an identity that feels correct for oneself but is considered abnormal or pathological by others. For example, there may have been a time early in life when your natal male child told a trusted adult that 'I'm really a girl' or 'I have the wrong body,' and was gently (or harshly) told 'No, you're a boy.' Perhaps it was explained that having a penis indicates decisively that one is a boy and not a girl. Those responses, even though well-intentioned, send an early message that it's not acceptable to be (or consider or talk about being) transgender.

As a result, it's difficult for transgender teens to be confident that what they know and feel inside is real. Some teens respond to this lack of confidence by adopting a rigid and demanding stance about transitioning. Some are plagued with self-doubt. Transgender teens need to feel supported in their exploration, without prejudgment. They must be free to try out whatever types of gender expression and identity feel comfortable and correct for them. They must be able to express and discuss their

---

4   *Counseling Transgender and Non-Binary Youth: The Essential Guide.* Irwin Krieger. Jessica Kingsley Publishers, 2017.

doubts without feeling this will be used against them when they reach certainty about their gender identity.

Mixed messages

While it is your role as a parent to raise safety concerns, you have to be careful about the mixed message in statements such as 'It's okay to dress as you like at home but not at school.' Often, transgender teens feel the need to try out authentic gender expression in public even if there may be a hostile response from peers and others. These teens are no longer willing to suppress their true selves for the sake of fitting in and being liked and getting treated better by others. Parents must work with the school and the community for this to be a safe and respected step for your child to take. This is better than simply accepting the belief that societal prejudice makes it too risky to proceed.

Learn from your own experiences

In your own life, did you honor and disclose something about yourself that others may have criticized or condemned? Did you keep an important part of your identity or desires secret in order to have others' approval? We can all recall facing this kind of dilemma at some point in our lives. Most of us find out that in the long run it is better to be true to ourselves and worry less about the responses of others. This is an especially tough challenge for teenagers, whether it's about clothes, music, unpopular interests or friends, sexuality, or gender identity and expression. We must do our best to support teens who are grappling with issues of authenticity, integrity, and societal disapproval. As the parent of a transgender teen, you must put aside, as best you can, your discomfort with your child's gender identity or unconventional gender expression.

Support your child

These tips will help you be supportive at this challenging time:

- Whenever possible, transgender teens need the company and support of other transgender teens and adults. Find out if there is a support group that your teen can join. To get started locating resources, contact an LGBT Community Center or see Appendix 1 of this book.
- Attend a support group for parents, or seek out an online parents' group.
- Go with your child to an LGBT youth conference, even if this requires some travel.
- Explore safe online support networks for LGBT teens.
- When your child meets other transgender teenagers, encourage them to keep in touch. Welcome these friends to visit in your home. Support them spending time together in ordinary teenage activities, even if this makes you a little uneasy. You'll get used to it! And your child will be much better off when you do. These friends' parents can be an additional support for you.

The next two chapters

In Chapter 7 we will look at the steps your family can take when your child has told you they are transgender. These include gathering information, getting an assessment and social transition steps which may then lead to medical intervention after some time. Medical interventions are discussed in Chapter 8.

7 Taking Steps

Knowledge and understanding

Your first step is to learn as much as you can about your child's gender identity and about transgender people in general. You must address each of the challenges you face when you contemplate that your child may be transgender, including any of those discussed in Chapter 5. Then listen with an open mind and an open heart to what your teen has to say about their own experience, their gender, and how they would like to proceed. Read as much as you can about being transgender, keeping in mind that your teen's experience is unique. There is not only one typical life path for a transgender person.[1] Look for any organizations, conferences or support groups in your area for transgender individuals and their families. See Appendix 1 for books, organizations and websites.

Counseling

A mental health professional who is knowledgeable about gender identity can be an enormous help to your child and your family. This gender identity specialist will be able to help you and your teen sort out the nature of their gender identity. Counseling will

---

1   Take a look at www.transpeoplespeak.org for videos of transgender people and their families discussing their experiences.

help you come to terms with any discomfort you have so you can offer full support. The gender identity specialist will also be able to help you decide about and navigate through any additional steps your child wants to take, especially if medical interventions are being considered. This will include referrals to local support groups, organizations and other health care providers, as well as suggestions about further reading and information about any conferences in your area for transgender teens and their parents.

A gender identity specialist will be familiar with the World Professional Association for Transgender Health *Standards of Care*.[2] The *Standards of Care* are the most widely accepted guidelines for the use of hormones or surgery for gender affirmation. One of the roles of this mental health clinician is to evaluate your teen's readiness for social transition, hormones or surgery. The gender identity specialist will explain to you and your teen the possible benefits and risks of each step. Benefits and risks of medical treatments will then be discussed in more detail with the medical provider.

These websites may help you find a therapist in your area who is experienced in the treatment of transgender people:

- Dr. Becky Allison: www.drbecky.com/therapists.html
- The Fenway Center provider list includes mental health and medical providers throughout the U.S., but especially in the Northeast: www.transcaresite.org
- TransPulse: www.lauras-playground.com/gender-therapists
- The World Professional Association for Transgender Health: www.wpath.org. From the home page click on 'find a provider' and search by location or specialty.

---

2   You can view the *Standards of Care* at www.wpath.org

If possible, it is best to verify independently that the therapist you find is fully credentialed and licensed. You can do this by speaking with a local health care provider.

Social transition

The next important and useful step is to support your teen in making a social transition. This is the point at which they are likely to request that you begin using a new name and new pronouns for them. You should do your best to always use their chosen name and pronouns. From a practical standpoint this is a difficult adjustment for parents, given the years of calling your child by the name you gave them and thinking of them as being fully in accord with their natal sex. And of course if you remain troubled or uncertain about your child's newly affirmed gender identity, or if the name you gave them has a special significance for you, it is difficult from an emotional standpoint as well.

A social transition happens when your teen chooses a moment to begin presenting in public as the person they feel themself to be. This may be a binary transition from living as a girl to living as a boy, or vice versa, or it may be a transition to affirming a non-binary gender identity. At first this may be limited to only at school, or in some other specific context, but eventually the social transition will be full time.

If your child affirms a non-binary identity, they will most likely ask you to refer to them with the pronouns 'they,' 'them,' 'their,' and 'themself.' Some young people prefer pronouns that have been created specifically for non-binary gender identity, such as the pronoun sets starting with 'ze' or 'xe.' Do your best to honor your child's pronoun request. As long as you have good intentions, your teen will understand that it may take a while for you to learn to use the new name and pronouns consistently.

You will be ready to endorse the social transition when you:

- feel fairly certain that your child should take this step to find out if their affirmed gender is authentic, or
- are aware that your child is in great distress over having to be identified by their assigned sex and you would like to give them the opportunity to experience some relief.

For most transgender teens, the primary challenges for social transition are at school and at extended family gatherings. One key indicator of readiness for a social transition is the child's sense that the relief they experience as a result of being true to themself will outweigh any harassment they may encounter. It is difficult to know in advance the amount of harassment your teen may experience. Many parents expect harassment to increase when a teenager makes a social transition. In my experience, however, many kids who had been harassed earlier for being gender nonconforming were treated better once they made a confident social transition. It seems that peers respond positively to the youth being more outgoing and self-assured in their affirmed gender. An increasingly androgynous presentation (changing hairstyle, jewelry, clothes and so on) by the teen prior to the transition will give you some ability to anticipate the likely level of harassment and plan accordingly.

The social transition at school
The following steps have helped my clients accomplish the social transition more smoothly at school:

- Your teen will begin by informing close friends. They will gradually dress in a more androgynous manner if they have not already done so. You will find that friends who have already shown themselves to be accepting of gays, lesbians, and gender nonconforming people are likely to be most supportive. If your teen had previously come out as gay or lesbian, they will already know which peers are open minded regarding these matters. (As mentioned in Chapter 3, some transgender people go through a phase of identifying as gay or lesbian.)

- Next, you and your teen will meet with school administrators (or perhaps first with a sympathetic teacher, nurse or school counselor) to request the transition. If there is a GSA (Gay Straight Alliance) or similar LGBT support organization at your child's school, the group's advisor is a good person to contact first. You and your teen will disclose the youth's transgender identity. You may have to explain to administrators what that means. You will ask the school to honor their affirmed gender and use their chosen name and pronouns.

- You will ask school administrators to take whatever steps they deem necessary to ensure more open mindedness about gender diversity in the school culture and to guarantee, to the greatest extent possible, that you child is safe at school and will be treated with respect. This may include diversity awareness presentations for students and/or faculty. If your school administration's response is unsatisfactory, call on one of the advocacy groups listed in Appendix 1. Any LGBT youth organizations in your region can also provide valuable assistance. It is the school administration's responsibility to ensure that teachers and students will be educated about gender diversity, that teachers will honor the student's gender identity, and that harassment will not be tolerated.

- Once your teen is attending school in their affirmed gender, word of mouth along with your teen's answers to any friendly questions will suffice to orient the rest of the student body to their new gender.
- Ideally your teen should be allowed to use the bathroom and locker room where they feel most comfortable, or to request a single bathroom and/or private changing room if they prefer. Schools are generally more comfortable with transgender students using single facilities, so it may take some advocacy on your part if your child prefers to use the group facilities.
- Team sports at the middle and high school level should be focused on education first and competition second.[3] Therefore, your child should be able to play on the team that fits their affirmed gender or, in the case of non-binary youth, the team where the teen feels they belong.

While this process for a social transition at school has worked repeatedly for the teens who have been my clients, it is important to discuss with your teen what approach would make them most comfortable. You should talk with the school administration (with sympathetic staff included in the discussion) about what steps they believe will achieve the smoothest transition. Then get ready to take it in your stride when your child's friends call them by their new name, or when you hear teachers using the new pronouns with ease.

You may discover that school personnel have many of the same fears and concerns you and other parents have experienced.

---

3   *Developing Policies for Transgender Students on High SchoolTeams.* Pat Griffin. National Federation of State High School Associations, 2015. Accessed on 3/1/17 at www.nfhs.org/articles/developingpolicies-for-transgender-students-on-high-school-teams

Be patient and persistent in encouraging them to address these fears and concerns. Ask them to keep in mind that your child's welfare depends on a successful social transition. If you encounter extreme hostility at any point in this process, you and your child may also decide that alternate schooling is the best and safest choice. It will not be good for your teen to abandon their authenticity if school becomes more difficult. If that should happen, just pull back, reassess your options, and find another way to move forward.

Informing family and friends

Telling the extended family and friends of the family is a stressful experience for most parents of transgender teens. Fear of rejection and criticism, or fear of causing unmanageable distress for older family members, is common. Many families keep this matter secret until a family or social gathering is coming. My recommendation to teens is that they defer to their parents, whenever possible, on when to notify relatives and adult family friends. My recommendation to parents is that they begin early on disclosing to close friends and family that their child is questioning gender identity. This lays the groundwork for a later disclosure of the new identity. As with your teen's disclosures, you will get the best responses from those who have already indicated in some way that they are open minded about LGBT people. Start with them first.

When it comes time for your child's social transition, it is important that you and your teen are in charge of how this information is shared with the extended family. In my experience, families have accomplished this by direct phone calls to each individual if the network is not that large, or by a letter or email if calling everyone is unmanageable. I do not recommend taking the short cut of asking one person to tell another, unless the intermediary knows your child well and is well-versed in information about gender identity.

By the time you are ready to send this letter, you will have gained some comfort and consistency in using your child's chosen name and pronouns. This will be reflected in the way you write your letter. You may want to include some or all of the following points in your letter:

- Tell family and friends that you would like them to receive some important news about your teen with an open mind. Let them know as simply and clearly as you can that you have learned something new about your child's identity. Share the new name and ask that they be respectful and make every effort to use this name and the corresponding pronouns when they speak to or about your child.

- Let them know if your child's affirmed gender was difficult for you to accept at first, and explain that you now know that this transition is best for your teen and will lead to the happiest outcome. You may add that this is something your teen has struggled with for a long time in silence. You are proud of your child's courage and glad they are finally able to be authentic. If there are improvements you have seen since the social transition started, mention them here.

- Stress that your teen is same person they have always been, with all of the same positive attributes you all value and love. (Don't hesitate to mention what those wonderful characteristics are!)

- Let them know that you welcome any questions they have about this change and that you look forward to telling them more about this if they would like to know more. You can also recommend this book to them so they can become more familiar with what it means to be transgender.

Be sure to review the letter with your teen before you send it out so they are comfortable with what you have written. Your teen may want to send a separate letter, or include a personal message in yours.

Here, as examples, are three sample letters. The first is the letter sent by Samantha's parents. (You met her as Sam in Chapter 3.) The second letter is from the parents of Marcus, who you met as Cassie in Chapter 4. In the third letter, Shane introduces themself to their grandparents.

Dear Family and Friends,

We are writing to share some news about our son, Sam. Over the last few years, Sam has been thinking a lot about who he really is, deep down inside. Last year Sam bravely told us that he feels he is a girl in a boy's body. As you can imagine, we were upset to hear this and didn't really understand. While Sam has always enjoyed feminine activities, we just accepted him as different from other boys. We knew he was a free spirit, a gentle and imaginative child. We never considered that he might not feel that he is a boy.

Well, now we do understand. We'd like to help you understand and support Sam as he embarks on the challenging journey of becoming Samantha. Sam has been going to school as Samantha. We've been very pleased with the response from teachers and classmates. We are getting used to friends calling the house and asking for 'Samantha.' We can see how happy and comfortable our child is now that she is living as a girl.

This has helped us feel good about supporting her transition to female in any way we can.

We know many challenges lie ahead for Samantha and for us. We ask you to approach this news with an open mind. Samantha would like you to use her new name from now on and to refer to her as 'she.' We have gradually learned to do so, although we occasionally slip up. This is a work-in-progress for all of us. Please continue to cherish and support her just as you did when she was a boy.

We are sending out this letter to get the discussion started. We look forward to having a chance to speak to you directly and answer any questions you may have.

Sincerely,
Donald and Michelle

Dear Friends and Family,

We have some news to share with you. There's been a big change in our family! Over the past year our easygoing Cassie had suddenly turned angry and uncooperative. We couldn't understand why until she told us that she really feels she is a boy and not a girl. It turns out she has been feeling out of place as a girl for a long time. This idea that Cassie is really a boy was hard for us to accept, and I imagine it will be hard for you, too.

Perhaps you have heard or read news stories about kids who are transgender, who make a transition at school from girl to boy or vice versa. We have been learning all about it since Cassie told us about herself. Since Cassie has accepted herself as transgender, she is back to being the same easygoing kid she always was—except now she is a smart, easygoing, athletic boy. His new name is Marcus. I hope you'll make the change to calling him Marcus and thinking of him as a boy, as we have. It definitely takes some practice! In fact, we're amazed that his friends and teachers are getting used to it, too.

We've met other transgender kids and their parents. It's been a big help to feel we're not alone with this. And now we want to invite you to be part of this big change in our lives. Please feel free to call or visit, to ask Marcus and us any questions you have. We're counting on your support!

Fondly,
Jen and Rob

Dear Grandma and Grandpa,

I know Mom told you about this a little bit but I want to tell you myself— My new name is Shane! I never felt I was one of the girls, and I know I'm not a boy either. I'm just me! I'm gender neutral, which means I'm not a girl and I'm not a boy. I hope you understand. I'm using 'they' pronouns. So when you talk about me, don't say, 'We have a granddaughter named Beth. She lives in New York with her parents. We're proud of her.' Say, 'We have a grandchild named Shane. They live in New York with their parents. We're proud of them for being true to themself.' And I hope you are! ☺

I can't wait to see you soon and I hope you still love me just the same!

Your loving grandchild,
Shane

Other steps in the social transition
A trans youth may request a legal name change when they feel certain of their intent to make a full and permanent transition.

This can generally be accomplished, with parental support, through your local probate court. If your teen has made a social transition and legal name change, their therapist can help provide documentation, per your state's regulations, to have the gender marker on the driver's license changed from female to male or vice versa. So far, Oregon, California and the District of Columbia are the only jurisdictions in the U.S. that allow a person to request to be listed as gender neutral on their license. Australia is the only country I know of that has a similar provision. Having identification that is consistent with gender presentation helps protect teenagers from harassment and keeps their transgender status private. The National Center for Transgender Equality (see Appendix 1) keeps up-to-date information on how to change federal and state documentation in the U.S.

Along with social transition, a trans girl who is well into male puberty may want to shave her body hair as well as any facial hair. As she becomes more certain that she is heading for female adulthood, she may also want to consider electrolysis or laser treatment for permanent removal of facial or body hair. She may request voice training to help her find a more female-sounding voice without straining. Some trans girls prefer to tuck their penis under to create the feel and appearance of more feminine genitals. A gaff is a garment used for this purpose. Gaffs can be homemade or purchased on the internet.

Non-binary youth assigned male at birth may want to consider these steps as well. The essential question is whether any of these steps will help them feel more at ease. The value to the youth may be in how it changes the way they feel and see themself. Or the importance of these steps may be in the way it changes how others view them.

For a trans boy, social transition will most likely include wearing a binder, which is a garment available for purchase online that flattens the breasts so he can more easily pass as a boy. He may also want to use a packer, which is placed in the underwear to create the feel and appearance of male genitals. Packers can be homemade or purchased on the internet.

A binder or a packer may also be used by a non-binary youth assigned female at birth. They may appreciate the way a binder lessens their sense of a female chest or the way it creates a more masculine profile. They may feel that a packer gives them the sense of male genitals or that it creates a more masculine look. As with so many of the choices contemplated by transgender youth, each of these components of social transition is a very personal decision.

8 Medical Transition

Hormones

There are two types of hormonal treatment that can be offered to teenagers: puberty-blocking hormones and cross-sex hormones. Puberty-blocking hormones are given to teens in the early stages of puberty who would like to delay puberty and who meet the criteria below:

- They have been gender nonconforming or they have expressed a transgender identity.
- They have had psychotherapy with a gender identity specialist.
- They have already made a social transition or feel that they are likely to want to do so.

These hormones suspend the bodily changes of puberty, giving the teen more time to decide on a future course. Cross-sex hormones are the second category of hormones. They help masculinize a female body or feminize a male body. They are given to teens with persistent gender dysphoria who want their body to conform more fully to their gender identity.

Puberty blockers for natal females

If your teen who was assigned female is treated with puberty blockers for a year or two and determines that his gender is male, he can then begin cross-sex hormone treatment with a better physical (male) outcome than if he had gone through female puberty before transitioning. Since he will be able to avoid breast development through the use of puberty-blocking hormones, he will not need to wear a binder or have breast removal surgery should he continue on the path toward male adulthood. Puberty blockers generally prevent the onset or continuation of menstruation. Teens and parents need to be aware that the teen who starts blockers very early in puberty and then goes directly to cross-sex hormones will not develop fertility. If, however, your teen concludes that she is *not* male, the puberty-blocking hormones will be discontinued and her body will proceed with its pubertal development, just delayed by the time on blockers.

Puberty blockers for natal males

If your teen who was assigned male is treated with puberty-blocking hormones for a year or two and determines that her gender is female, she can initiate cross-sex hormones with a better physical (female) outcome than if she had gone through male puberty before transitioning. The pitch of her voice will not become deeper once blockers are started, nor will she develop additional facial hair. Her face will not become more masculine, so she will be less likely to need facial feminization surgery as an adult if she is concerned about passing easily as female. Again, teens and parents need to be aware that the teen who starts blockers very early in puberty and then goes directly to cross-sex hormones will not develop fertility. If, however, your teen concludes that he is *not* female, the puberty-blocking hormones will be discontinued and his body will proceed with its pubertal development, just delayed by the time on blockers.

Cross-sex hormones for natal females
Cross-sex hormones (primarily testosterone for masculinization) allow the body of your child assigned female at birth to conform more closely to his male gender identity. While the *Standards of Care* and the Endocrine Society Guidelines[1] recommend cross-sex hormones for teens who are 16 years and older, many transgender health care centers in the U.S. that treat adolescents now recommend that this treatment be offered at younger ages when appropriate for the teen.[2,3,4] Many transgender teens feel some emotional relief immediately upon starting to take cross-sex hormones, although the desired changes (facial hair, lower voice and increased upper body strength) will take some months to begin and a number of years to reach completion. Menstruation generally stops within a few months.

Taking cross-sex hormones creates certain medical risks and may lead to infertility. These are matters which the teen and his parents must discuss with their therapist before a referral is made to an endocrinologist or other medical provider knowledgeable

1   'Endocrine treatment of gender-dysphoric/gender-incongruent persons: An Endocrine Society clinical practice guideline.' W.C. Hembree, P.T. Cohen-Kettenis, L.J. Gooren, S.E. Hannema, W.J. Meyer, M.H. Murad, S.M. Rosenthal, J.D. Safer, V. Tangpricha, and G.G. T'Sjoen. *Journal of Clinical Endocrinology & Metabolism*, 102:11, 2017, pp.3869–3903.

2   'Approach to the patient: Transgender youth: Endocrine considerations.' S. Rosenthal. *Journal of Clinical Endocrinology and Metabolism*, 99:12, 2014, pp.4379–4389.

3   'Management of the transgender adolescent.' J. Olson, C. Forbes and M. Belzer. *Archives of Pediatric Adolescent Medicine*, 165:2, 2011, pp.171–176.

4   'Multidisciplinary care for gender-diverse youth: A narrative review and unique model of gender-affirming care.' D. Chen, M. Hidalgo, S. Leibowitz, J. Leininger, L. Simons, C. Finlayson and R. Garofalo. *Transgender Health*, 1:1, 2016, pp.117–123.

about cross-sex hormones. These concerns will be discussed further with the medical provider and relevant lab tests will be done before your teen can start taking hormones.

Your teen will have to take cross-sex hormones throughout his life if he wants all of the changes caused by the hormones to persist. The medical risks will also persist as long as he is taking hormones. Therefore it is essential that your child maintains regular medical visits and completes all lab tests as requested to maintain the highest level of medical safety. It is important to take the prescribed dose exactly as directed by the doctor. It is not safe to seek hormones without a doctor's prescription. Your teen's therapist will help you and your teen think through the hormone options, clarify when hormone treatment may be indicated, and make a referral to an appropriate endocrine provider at your request.

Cross-sex hormones may also be prescribed when requested by teens who are transitioning to a non-binary identity.[5] This also requires discussion between the teen, parents, therapist and endocrine provider before treatment is offered. Some non-binary teens are prescribed cross-sex hormones at lower doses or for a limited time rather than long term.

Cross-sex hormones for natal males

Cross-sex hormones (primarily estrogen for feminization) allow the body of your child assigned male at birth to conform more closely to her female gender identity. While the *Standards of Care* and the Endocrine Society Guidelines recommend cross-sex hormones for teens aged 16 or older, many transgender health

---

5   *Approach to Genderqueer, Gender Non-Conforming, and Gender Nonbinary People.* Jennifer Hastings. Center of Excellence for Transgender Health, University of California, San Francisco, 2016. Accessed on 3/1/17 at www.transhealth.ucsf.edu/trans?page=guidelines-gendernonconforming

care centers that treat adolescents now recommend that this treatment be offered at younger ages when appropriate for the teen (see footnotes 2–4). Many transgender teens feel some emotional relief immediately upon starting to take cross-sex hormones, although the desired changes (breast development, fuller hips and softer skin) will take some time to begin and a number of years to reach completion. Electrolysis or laser hair removal can be considered for teens with significant facial or body hair, along with or prior to taking cross-sex hormones.

Taking cross-sex hormones creates certain medical risks and may lead to infertility. These are matters which the teen and her parents must discuss with their therapist before a referral is made to an endocrinologist or other medical provider knowledgeable about cross-sex hormones. These concerns will be discussed further with the medical provider and relevant lab tests will be done before your teen can start taking hormones.

Your teen will have to take cross-sex hormones throughout her life if she wants all of the changes caused by the hormones to persist. The medical risks will also persist as long as she is taking hormones. Therefore it is essential that your child maintains regular medical visits and completes all lab tests as requested to maintain the highest level of medical safety. It is important to take the prescribed dose exactly as directed by the doctor. It is not safe to seek hormones without a doctor's prescription. Your child's gender identity specialist will help you and your teen think through the hormone options, clarify when hormone treatment may be indicated, and make a referral to an appropriate endocrine provider at your request.

Cross-sex hormones may also be prescribed when requested by teens who are transitioning to a non-binary identity (see footnote 5). This also requires discussion among the teen, parents, therapist and endocrine provider before treatment is offered.

Some non-binary teens are prescribed cross-sex hormones at lower doses or for a limited time rather than long term.

Impatient teens

Many transgender teens are exceedingly anxious to begin taking hormones, long before their parents have enough information to consider such a request, or the confidence that such intervention is right for their child. You will have to ask your teen to be patient as you take the time you need to understand their identity and needs, and the realities of hormonal intervention. In most cases, a three- or six-month delay in starting hormones will not make an appreciable difference in long-term outcome. (Exceptions to this would be a teen experiencing rapid pubertal change or a student who wants to start hormones during senior year of high school to be able to pass better in their affirmed gender at college.) I often point out to impatient teens that they are well ahead of the pack in that they have reached a clear understanding of their gender discordance and have parents who are engaged in this process with them. Many trans people have had to wait well into adulthood to have the understanding and resources to transition, and many have done so without any support or acceptance from their families.

Surgery

A teen who requests surgery prior to age 18 will generally need parental agreement and support (financial and otherwise). The most common surgery sought by teens is 'top surgery' (double mastectomy and male chest reconstruction) for people transitioning from female to male or, in some cases, female to non-binary. This surgery relieves the trans boy who has made a social transition from having to continue to use a binder and keep his chest covered all summer. He no longer has to walk stooped over or wear loose, layered clothes to hide his breasts. For parents, the idea of this surgery can be quite distressing, even if it is something your child is anxious to undergo.

It is important to take the time you need to understand that your child who is requesting top surgery is extremely uncomfortable about having female breasts. It may help if you imagine how a cisgender male child would feel if he developed breasts in puberty. (In fact, surgery is offered for cisgender males who develop breast tissue.) While your teen may be happy about the prospect of surgery, you may need time to grieve the loss of a cherished daughter. Keep in mind that most of the things you value and admire about your teen will be unchanged. The most likely outcome for a youth after top surgery is to feel happier, more at ease, and more comfortable with a male chest.

Facial feminization surgery (often abbreviated as FFS) is sought by some trans women whose facial structure has masculinized in puberty. Because of continued bone development in young adulthood, FFS is not recommended prior to age 19 or 20. An experienced surgeon can provide a consultation at that time about developmental readiness and the visual changes that can be accomplished with surgery. FFS to date is not covered by health insurance, while hormone treatments, top surgery, and genital surgeries are covered by those plans that include transgender health care as a benefit. Some trans women also seek surgical breast augmentation if their breast development with hormone treatment is not satisfactory. They are recommended to complete at least one or two years of cross-sex hormone treatment before considering this surgery.

Genital surgeries, sometimes referred to as 'bottom surgeries,' are generally restricted to people over age 18, although some surgeons in the U.S. have provided these surgeries at age 17. These include genital reconstruction (removal of the penis and testicles and creation of a vagina, clitoris and labia for natal males, as well as a number of procedures for transition from female to male genitalia) and the removal of female reproductive organs. For parents, the idea of genital surgery may be very disturbing, even if it is something your child deeply desires. Generally, transgender people who pursue genital surgery are extremely uncomfortable about having genitals that are not in accord with their gender identity. As these surgeries are steps which your young person is likely to take only in adulthood, your role as a parent in the process will be different than it is for the transition steps your child seeks as a teen.

Conclusion

Now it's time to take a deep breath and reflect on all you have read here. It will also be helpful to talk things over with your spouse or partner, close friends or family, and your child. You may want to confer with a mental health professional or clergy. Thinking about surgery can be especially upsetting, so let go of that for now.

Focus on what's most important at this time:

- Keep an open mind about the validity and meaning of your child's inner experience. Remember that keeping an open mind about what your child is telling you keeps the lines of communication open.
- Examine your fears and concerns. It is natural for parents, because of their fears and concerns, to have a bias against believing that a child may be transgender. It is also hard to believe that something this important in your child's life could have been unknown to you. But if your first response is to strongly oppose what your teen is saying about gender identity, they are more likely to adopt a stubborn, oppositional point of view in future discussions.
- Listen, ask questions, be flexible, be patient.

It is wonderful for your child that you are willing to face this difficult situation head on. I know you want to be the best support you can be for your teen. You also want to keep your child safe. At times your child may be impatient and angry with you for having doubts or taking too much time. At those times, be sure to appreciate your own efforts, and your willingness to proceed on this challenging path. With an open mind, compassion and perseverance, you and your teen will find your way to a positive outcome.

Appendix 1 of this book provides a list of resources to help you gain a greater understanding of your teen. It includes organizations you can turn to for support for yourself and for your child as you begin this journey. Remember to take your time and to take advantage of all of the resources available. Remember, also, that many other families have faced these challenges with remarkably good outcomes.

I am continually inspired by transgender people. They are willing to overcome tremendous obstacles in order to be completely true to themselves. I hope this book will help you appreciate and support your transgender teen in their struggle to achieve full authenticity.

Resources for Parents of Transgender Teens

An updated list of resources and contact information for Irwin Krieger can be found at www.HelpingYourTransgenderTeen.com

---

SUPPORT AND ADVOCACY ORGANIZATIONS IN THE U.S.
(see below for legal advocacy groups)

Black Trans Advocacy (www.blacktrans.org) is the leading national resource working to advance black transgender equality. They are active in 14 states providing local community building and support, public education and training, mentoring and referral to program services. Check the website for locations.

Campus Pride (www.campuspride.org) serves LGBTQ and ally student leaders and campus organizations to create safer, more inclusive LGBTQ-friendly colleges and universities. The Campus Pride Index (campusprideindex.org) is a free online database of LGBTQ-friendly campuses.

GLSEN (originally: The Gay, Lesbian and Straight Education Network) (www.glsen.org) is the largest national education organization working to ensure safe schools for all students.

National Center for Transgender Equality (www.transequality. org) is the leading social justice advocacy organization in the U.S. for transgender people.

PFLAG (originally: Parents and Friends of Lesbians and Gays) (www.pflag.org) is the largest family and ally organization in the U.S., uniting people who are lesbian, gay, bisexual, transgender, and queer (LGBTQ) with families, friends, and allies.

Transactive (www.transactiveonline.org) offers training, advocacy, family support and other resources to benefit gender diverse and transgender children, adolescents, young adults, their families and the communities in which they live.

Transathlete (www.transathlete.com) is a resource for students, athletes, coaches, and administrators to find information about trans inclusion in athletics.

TransKids Purple Rainbow Foundation (www. transkidspurplerainbow.org) provides education and advocacy along with supports for trans youth.

TransParent (www.transparentusa.org) has support groups for parents with transgender children in four states and the District of Columbia. Check the website for locations.

The Trans Youth Equality Foundation (TYEF) (www. transyouthequality.org) provides education, advocacy and support for transgender and gender nonconforming children and youth and their families.

Trans Youth Family Allies (TYFA) (www.imatyfa.org) empowers children and families by partnering with educators, service providers, and communities, to develop supportive environments in which gender may be expressed and respected.

LEGAL ADVOCACY GROUPS IN THE U.S.

GLAD
www.glad.org

Lambda Legal
www.lambdalegal.org

National Center for Lesbian Rights
www.nclrights.org/our-work/transgender-law

Sylvia Rivera Law Project
www.srlp.org

Transgender Law and Policy Institute
www.transgenderlaw.org

Transgender Law Center
www.transgenderlawcenter.org

Transgender Legal Defense and Education Fund
www.transgenderlegal.org

PHONE AND ONLINE CRISIS SUPPORT FOR LGBT YOUTH IN THE U.S. AND CANADA

GLBT National Help Center (U.S.)
www.glnh.org or (888) 843-4564.

Trans Lifeline
www.translifeline.org. U.S.: (877) 565-8860 and Canada: (877) 330-6366.

Trevor Project (U.S.)
www.thetrevorproject.org (888-4-U-TREVOR) is a confidential 24/7 crisis and suicide prevention helpline for LGBT youth.

Youthline (Canada)
Open from 16:00–21:30 Sunday–Friday (Toronto time zone). Call: (800) 268-9688. Text: (647) 694-4275. TTY: (416) 962-0777. Email: askus@youthline.ca. To chat, go to www.youthline.ca and click the Chat button at the top of the page.

YOUTH AND FAMILY CONFERENCES IN THE U.S.

Black Trans Advocacy, Dallas
www.blacktrans.org/conference/btac-welcome.html

First Event, Boston
www.firstevent.org

Gender Conference East
www.genderconferenceeast.org

Gender Infinity, Houston
www.genderinfinity.org

Gender Odyssey, Seattle
www.genderodyssey.org

Gender Spectrum, California
www.genderspectrum.org

Philadelphia Trans Health Conference
www.mazzonicenter.org/trans-health

True Colors LGBT Youth Conference, Connecticut
www.ourtruecolors.org

CONFERENCES OUTSIDE THE U.S.

International Lesbian, Gay, Bisexual, Trans and Intersex Association
www.ilga.org

Sparkle (UK)
www.sparkle.org.uk

Trans*-Tagung Muenchen (Germany)
www.transtagung-muenchen.com

Transguys.com
Keeps a comprehensive list of conferences worldwide.

WPATH
www.wpath.org has information on international and regional conferences.

SUMMER CAMPS IN THE U.S.

Camp Aranu'tiq
www.camparanutiq.org is a summer camp in New Hampshire.

Get Free
www.bgdblog.org is a summer program for queer and trans youth of color in Oakland, California.

Trans Youth Equality Foundation
www.transyouthequality.org holds summer and fall retreats in Maine.

ONLINE SUPPORT FOR PARENTS AND YOUTH

Gender Spectrum Lounge (www.genderspectrum.org/lounge) is an online space for teens, parents, and professionals to connect with one another. Members can form their own groups and participate in a broader online community.

TransFamily (www.transfamily.org/discussion.html) has a moderated online discussion group for parents and a separate group for youth.

Trevor Space (www.trevorspace.org) is a monitored social and peer networking site for LGBT youth aged 13–24.

COUNSELING

These websites may help you find a therapist in your area who is experienced in the treatment of transgender youth:

- Dr. Becky Allison: www.drbecky.com/therapists.html
- The Fenway Center provider list includes mental health and medical providers throughout the U.S., but especially in the Northeast: www.transcaresite.org
- Transpulse: www.lauras-playground.com/gender-therapists
- The World Professional Association for Transgender Health: www.wpath.org. From the home page click on 'find a provider' and search by location or specialty.

If possible, it is best to verify independently that the therapist you find is fully credentialed and licensed. You can do this by speaking with a local health care provider.

MEDICAL INFORMATION

**Australian and New Zealand Association
for Transgender Health**
www.anzpath.org

Center of Excellence for Transgender Health (U.S.)
www.transhealth.ucsf.edu

European Professional Association for Transgender Health
www.epath.eu

Fenway Center (U.S.)
www.transcaresite.org

Gender Identity Research and Education Society (UK)
www.gires.org.uk

Transgender ASIA Research Centre
www.transgenderasia.org

Vancouver Coastal Health (Canada)
www.transhealth.vch.ca

World Professional Association for Transgender Health
www.wpath.org

ORGANIZATIONS OUTSIDE THE U.S.
AFRICA
Iranti-org
www.iranti-org.co.za

ASIA
Asia-Pacific Transgender Network
www.weareaptn.org

AUSTRALIA
Gender Centre, Inc.
www.gendercentre.org.au

Transcend Support
www.transcendsupport.com.au

True Colours
www.truecolours.org.au

CANADA
Gender Creative Kids
www.gendercreativekids.ca

PFLAG Canada
www.pflagcanada.ca/pflag-chapters

CARIBBEAN AND LATIN AMERICA
REDLACTRANS
www. redlactrans.org.ar/site

CUBA
CENESEX
www.cenesex.org

EUROPE
Transgender Europe
www.tgeu.org

INDIA
Sahodari Foundation
www.sahodari.org

IRELAND
Transgender Equality Network Ireland
www.teni.ie

SOUTH AFRICA
Gender Dynamix
www.genderdynamix.org.za

SWITZERLAND
Transgender Network Switzerland
www.transgender-network.ch

UNITED KINGDOM
Gendered Intelligence
www.genderedintelligence.co.uk

Mermaids
www.mermaidsuk.org.uk

Scottish Trans Alliance
www.scottishtrans.org

trans*formation
www.transformationuk.com

GLOBAL ORGANIZATIONS
FTM International
www.ftmi.org

Global Action for Trans* Equality
www.transactivists.org

OutRight Action International
www.outrightinternational.org

PUBLICATIONS AVAILABLE ONLINE

Available from American Civil Liberties Union, Gender
Spectrum, Human Rights Campaign, National Center
for Lesbian Rights and National Education Association at
www.nclrights.org:

- *Schools in Transition: A Guide for Supporting Transgender
  Students in K-12 Schools.*

Available from Family Acceptance Project in English, Spanish,
and Chinese at www.familyproject.sfsu.edu/publications:

- *Supportive Families, Healthy Children: Helping Families
  with Lesbian, Gay, Bisexual & Transgender Children.*

Available from GLSEN at www.glsen.org:

- *Model District Policy on Transgender and Gender Nonconforming Students*
- *Safe Space Kit*
- Resources for educators including *LGBT-Inclusive Curriculum.*

Available from GSA Network at www.gsanetwork.org:

- *Beyond the Binary: A Toolkit for Gender Identity Activism in Schools.*

Available from Human Rights Campaign at www.hrc.org:

- *Safer Sex for Trans Bodies.*

Available from Lambda Legal at www.lambdalegal.org:

- *Bathrooms and Locker Rooms: Understanding Your Rights*
- *Bending the Mold: An Action Kit for Transgender Students*
- *How Schools Can Support Transgender Students.*

Available from Latina at www.latina.com:

- *Coming Out as Transgender to Your Latino Family: Tips from a Trans Latina Counselor.*

Available from National LGBTQ Task Force (bilingual Spanish and English) at www.thetaskforce.org/static_html/downloads/release_materials/tf_a_la_familia.pdf:

- *A La Familia: Una Conversación Sobre Nuestras Familias, La Biblia, La Orientación Sexual y la Identidad de Género.*

Available from Scientific American Mind at www.scientificamerican.com:

- *Transgender Kids: What Does It Take to Help Them Thrive?* by Francine Russo.

Available from Transgender Youth Equality Foundation at www.transyouthequality.org/for-parents:

- Links to videos and other resources for parents.

BOOKS FOR PARENTS

Artistic Expressions of Transgender Youth by Tony Ferraiolo, 2015.

Becoming Nicole: The Transformation of an American Family by Amy Ellis Nutt, Random House, 2016.

The Conscious Parent's Guide to Gender Identity: A Mindful Approach to Embracing Your Child's Authentic Self by Darlene Tando, Adams Media, 2016.

Counseling Transgender and Non-Binary Youth: The Essential Guide by Irwin Krieger, Jessica Kingsley Publishers, 2017.

The Gender Creative Child: Pathways for Nurturing and Supporting Children Who Live Outside of Gender Boxes by Diane Ehrensaft, The Experiment, 2016.

The Lives of Transgender People by Genny Beemyn and Susan Rankin, Columbia University Press, 2011.

Now What? A Handbook for Families with Transgender Children by Rex Butt, Transgress Press, 2015.

The Sexual Spectrum: Why We're All Different by Olive Skene Johnson, Raincoast Books, 2004.

Trans Bodies, Trans Selves: A Resource for the Transgender Community, edited by Laura Erickson-Schroth, Oxford University Press, 2014.

Transgender 101: A Simple Guide to a Complex Issue by Nicholas Teich, Columbia University Press, 2012.

The Transgender Child: A Handbook for Families and Professionals by Stephanie Brill and Rachel Pepper, Cleis Press, 2008.

Transgender Children and Youth: Cultivating Pride and Joy with Families in Transition by Elijah C. Nealy, W.W. Norton & Company, 2017.

Transgender Family Law: An Effective Guide to Advocacy, edited by Jennifer Levi and Elizabeth Monnin-Browder, Author House, 2012.

The Transgender Teen: A Handbook for Parents and Professionals Supporting Transgender and Non-Binary Teens by Stephanie Brill and Lisa Kenney, Cleis Press, 2016.

Transitions of the Heart: Stories of Love, Struggle and Acceptance by Mothers of Transgender and Gender Variant Children, edited by Rachel Pepper, Cleis Press, 2012.

'You're in the Wrong Bathroom!' And 20 Other Myths and Misconceptions About Transgender and Gender-Nonconforming People by Laura Erickson-Schroth and Laura A. Jacobs, Beacon Press, 2017.

BOOKS FOR TEENS

Gender Quest Workbook: A Guide for Teens and Young Adults Exploring Gender Identity by Rylan J. Testa, Deborah Coolheart and Jayme Peta, Instant Help, 2015.

Trans Bodies, Trans Selves: A Resource for the Transgender Community, edited by Laura Erickson-Schroth, Oxford University Press, 2014.

TEEN NOVELS

A Boy Like Me by Jennie Woods, 215 Ink, 2014.

Being Emily by Rachel Gold, Bella Books, 2012.

George by Alex Gino, Scholastic, Inc., 2017.

I am J by Cris Beam, Little, Brown Books for Young Readers, 2012.

If I Was Your Girl by Meredith Russo, Flatiron Books, 2016.

Luna by Julie Anne Peters, Little, Brown and Company, 2004.

Parrotfish by Ellen Wittlinger, Simon and Schuster, 2007.

TEEN MEMOIRS

Being Jazz: My Life as a (Transgender) Teen by Jazz Jennings, Crown Books for Young Readers, 2016.

Beyond Magenta: Transgender Teens Speak Out, edited by Susan Kuklin, Walker Books Ltd, 2015.

Rethinking Normal: A Memoir in Transition by Katie Rain Hill, Simon & Schuster Books for Young Readers, 2015.

Some Assembly Required: The Not-So-Secret Life of a Transgender Teen by Arin Andrew, Simon & Schuster Books for Young Readers, 2015.

ADULT MEMOIRS

Becoming a Visible Man by Jamison Green, Vanderbilt University Press, 2004.

He's Always Been My Son: A Mother's Story About Raising Her Transgender Son by Janna Barkin, Jessica Kingsley Publishers, 2017.

Just Add Hormones: An Insider's Guide to the Transsexual Experience by Matt Kailey, Beacon Press, 2005.

Nina Here Nor There: My Journey Beyond Gender by Nick Krieger, Beacon Press, 2011.

Redefining Realness: My Path to Womanhood, Identity, Love & So Much More by Janet Mock, Atria, 2014.

Second Son: Transitioning Toward My Destiny, Love and Life by Ryan K. Sallans, Title Town, 2012.

She's Not There: A Life in Two Genders by Jennifer Finney Boylan, Broadway Books, 2013.

The Testosterone Files: My Hormonal and Social Transformation from FEMALE to MALE by Max Wolf Valerio, Seal Press, 2006.

Transparent: Love, Family, and Living the T with Transgender Teenagers by Cris Beam, Harcourt, Inc., 2007.

Trading Places: When Our Son Became a Daughter by Jane Baker, Braefield Press, LLC, 2014.

Glossary

Affirmed gender is an individual's declared gender identity.

An **agender** person feels they have no gender.

Androgynous presentation includes both masculine and feminine elements.

Assigned sex, female or male, is determined at birth, based on the appearance of the baby's genitals.

Autism spectrum disorders (ASDs) include a wide range of conditions that affect a person's social interactions and communication. Some people with ASD engage in repetitive behaviors or have fixated interests.

A **bigender** person feels they have two genders.

A **binder** is a garment used to flatten the chest. It helps the individual be less aware of their breasts and present a more masculine body profile.

Bisexual individuals feel love and sexual attraction toward males and females.

Cisgender individuals' assigned sex, gender identity and gender expression are either all male or all female.

Coming out is the process of telling others that one is gay, lesbian, bisexual, or transgender.

Cross-sex hormones cause a male body to become more feminine or a female body to become more masculine.

Crossdressers wish to adopt the clothing and styles of grooming typical, in their culture, of the other sex.

Electrolysis is a treatment to remove unwanted facial or body hair.

An **endocrinologist** is a physician specializing in the body's production of hormones, including those that make a person more masculine or feminine. *Endocrine providers* for trans youth may include other physicians, physician assistants, or advanced practice nurses.

Facial feminization surgery (FFS) is surgery to make a masculine face appear feminine.

A **female-to-male (FTM)** person was assigned female at birth, is considered by others to be female, but feels male. He wants to have a masculine body and to be viewed by others as male.

A **gaff** is a garment designed to keep male genitals tucked under. It helps the individual be less aware of their genitals and present a more feminine body profile.

Gay is a common term for homosexual.

Gay men are men who love and are sexually attracted to men.

Gender dysphoria is a clinical term used to describe the unhappiness or distress caused by a discordance between gender identity and assigned sex or by societal expectations for that sex.

Gender expression is a person's presentation of self to others as masculine, feminine, neither, or both.

Gender identity is a person's inner sense of being female, male, neither, or both.

A **gender identity specialist** is a mental health professional with expertise about gender identity and expression.

Gender nonconforming kids are those whose desires, behaviors, and manner do not conform to societal expectations for children of their assigned sex.

Genderfluid, **genderqueer** and **gender neutral** people are those with a gender identity that is neither male nor female, or whose gender identity is a blend of male and female.

Heterosexual individuals feel love and sexual attraction toward members of the opposite sex.

Homosexual individuals feel love and sexual attraction toward members of the same sex.

Intersex people are those who are born with both male and female sex characteristics. These may include their genitals, hormones, and/or chromosomes.

LGBT is an abbreviation for lesbian, gay, bisexual, and transgender.

Lesbians are women who love and are sexually attracted to women.

A **male-to-female (MTF)** person was assigned male at birth, is considered by others to be male, but feels female. She wants to have a feminine body and to be viewed by others as female.

To **misgender** is to refer to someone by a name, pronoun, or gendered word (e.g., son, daughter) that does not fit with the individual's affirmed gender.

Natal sex is another term that can be used for the sex assigned at birth. A person may be referred to as a *natal female* or a *natal male*.

Non-binary gender identities are those that fall outside the gender categories of female and male. Some examples are: genderqueer, gender neutral, genderfluid, pangender, polygender, third gender, transmasculine, and transfeminine.

A **packer** is placed in the pants or underwear to create the feeling and appearance of male genitals.

Glossary

Pangender and **polygender** people affirm a gender identity that encompasses more than female and male genders.

Pansexual individuals feel love and sexual attraction toward others without placing importance on the partner's sex or gender.

Puberty is the stage of physical development when an individual's body undergoes sexual maturation.

Puberty-blocking hormones postpone the onset or completion of puberty.

Sex, female or male, is assigned at birth based on the appearance of the baby's genitals.

Sexuality refers to sexual feelings and behaviors.

Social transition is the time when a transgender person begins presenting in public according to their gender identity rather than according to their assigned sex.

Straight is a common term for a heterosexual cisgender person.

Third-gender people affirm a gender identity other than female or male.

Trans is an acceptable, shortened form of *transgender*.

Transfeminine individuals' gender identity and expression are in the female/feminine region of the spectrum but they do not necessarily identify as female.

Transgender people have a gender identity and/or gender expression that does not conform to their assigned sex.

Transmasculine individuals' gender identity and expression are in the male/masculine region of the spectrum but they do not necessarily identify as male.

Transsexual is a term that has been used to describe people whose gender identity is in sharp contrast to their assigned sex (as opposed to those with a non-binary identity). This term is now used less often, and is not generally used by teens.

Index

Irwin Krieger, LCSW is a clinical social worker in Connecticut who has provided psychotherapy for LGBT individuals, couples, and families for over 30 years. In addition to working in private practice, he was on the mental health team at AIDS Project New Haven from 2004 to 2015. He was a 2013 recipient of the New Haven Pride Center's Dorothy Award for his service to the LGBT community in New Haven. He is the 2017 recipient of the National Association of Social Workers Connecticut Chapter's Lifetime Achievement Award.

Since 2004, Irwin has worked extensively with transgender teens and adults and their families, as a therapist and a clinical supervisor. With the goal of expanding the base of knowledgeable providers for transgender individuals, Irwin provides training and consultation for mental health and health care professionals, as well as school personnel. He has presented at the World Professional Association for Transgender Health Symposium in Atlanta, the Philadelphia Trans Health Conference, Boston Children's Hospital, the Maine Academy of Family Physicians, Yale University, and the University of Connecticut. From 2012 to 2016 he was a consultant for the Transgender Care Team at Yale Health Plan. Irwin Krieger is the author of *Counseling Transgender and Non-Binary Youth: The Essential Guide*, also by JKP.

For more information on Irwin and his work, visit www.IKriegerTraining.com.